THE OFFICIAL RSPCA PET GUIDE

Care for Your

Rabbit

D0530671

CONTENTS

HarperCollins*Publishers*

First published in 1980 by
William Collins Sons & Co Ltd, London
New edition published in 1990

Reprinted by HarperCollins Publishers 1991, 1992, 1994 (twice),
1995 (twice), 1996, 1997 (twice), 1998

This is a fully revised and extended edition of *Care for your Rabbit*, first
published in 1980 and reprinted 14 times

© Royal Society for the Prevention of Cruelty to Animals 1980, 1990

Text of the 1980 edition by Tina Hearne; text revisions and additions for
this edition by Margaret Crush

Designed and edited by The Templar Company plc
Pippbrook Mill, London Road, Dorking, Surrey RH4 1JE

Front cover photograph: Animal Ark, London
Text photographs: Animal Photography Ltd, British Rabbit Council,
Bruce Coleman Ltd, Fox Photos, C & L Nature (Cyril Laubscher),
Sue Streeter, Diana Wyllie, ZEFA

Illustrations: Bob Hersey/Bernard Thornton Artists

**A catalogue record for this book is available
from the British Library**

ISBN 0 00 412546 0

Printed in Hong Kong by Sing Cheong Printing Co. Ltd.

First things first, animals are fun. Anybody who has ever enjoyed the company of a pet knows well enough just how strong the bond between human and animal can be. Elderly or lonely people often depend on a pet for their only company, and this can be a rewarding relationship for both human and animal. Doctors have proved that animals can be instrumental in the prevention of and recovery from mental or physical disease. Children learn the meaning of loyalty, unselfishness and friendship by growing up with animals.

But the commitment to an animal doesn't begin and end with a visit to the local pet shop. A pet should never be given as a 'surprise' present. The decision to bring a pet into your home should always be discussed and agreed by all the members of your family. Bear in mind that parents are ultimately responsible for the health and well-being of the animal for the whole of its lifetime. If you are not prepared for the inevitable expense, time, patience and occasional frustration involved, then the RSPCA would much rather that you didn't have a pet.

Armed with the facts, aware of the pitfalls but still confident of your ability to give a pet a good home, the next step is to find where you can get an animal from. Seek the advice of a veterinary surgeon or RSPCA Inspector about reputable local breeders or suppliers. Do consider the possibility of offering a home to an animal from an RSPCA establishment. There are no animals more deserving of loving owners.

As for the care of your pet, you should find in this book all you need to know to keep it happy, healthy and rewarding for many years to come. Responsible ownership means happy pets. Enjoy the experience!

Terence C. Bate

TERENCE BATE BVSc, LLB, MRCVS
Chief Veterinary Officer, RSPCA

Introduction

However cuddly, appealing and irresistible a young rabbit appears in the pet shop, it is not an animated toy but a living creature with specific requirements. It will need time and attention daily if it is to stay happy and healthy. Like any pet spending part of its life in captivity, a rabbit deserves the very best care and attention its owner can give it.

So, before acquiring any rabbit, it is important to consider the following ten basic facts, to make sure a rabbit is the right pet to choose, and that it and its owner will be happy together.

1   Rabbits need feeding twice a day, *every* day.
2   Hutches must be cleaned out regularly.
3   Rabbits are relatively cheap to feed, but they need good, secure housing and, unless a hutch can be made, a bought one is not cheap.
4   In the wild, rabbits live in colonies and need companionship, so, ideally, no pet rabbit should be kept alone. If the rabbit *must* live without the company of another rabbit, its owner must spend much time with it, and/or give it the companionship of another animal such as a guinea pig.
5   All rabbits need daily exercise, preferably in a safe, grassy area.
6   It is important not to breed from a rabbit unless good homes can definitely be found for its young.
7   Someone must look after the rabbit while the owner goes on holiday.
8   A rabbit is basically a healthy creature, but if it becomes ill, the owner must be willing to pay for a consultation with the vet.
9   After a few months children may well become bored with their pet rabbit, so an adult will have to be responsible for its daily needs.
10 It is important to choose a breed of the right size and weight. Some breeds may be too big for children to handle with confidence and safety. Small and medium breeds are best.

A well-cared for rabbit, given the freedom of a sizeable run or a secure part of the garden, makes a lively, responsive and delightful pet.

Varieties

Tame rabbits were originally bred from the wild: some for fur; some for meat; others for the show bench. Keeping them as pets is a more recent hobby, well-served by the diversity of choice available.

Pure-bred rabbits fall into three distinct categories: normal fur breeds, with the same kind of coat as the wild rabbit; the fancy or novelty breeds, created primarily for the show bench; and the Rex and Satin breeds, characterized by the particular qualities of their fur. However, if a pet is wanted and not a show animal, a cross-bred rabbit can often be as attractive and hardier.

NORMAL FUR BREEDS

The normal fur breeds have short, soft underhair, interspersed with longer, stiffer guard hairs. Some, such as the Californian and the New Zealand White, have been bred for meat; most have been bred for their fur, and as their breed names suggest, some have coats that simulate those of other animals. These rabbits include the Silver Fox, the Sable and the Chinchilla, whose fur is sometimes said to surpass that of the animal it imitates. The Havana has a rich chocolate-coloured coat that looks not unlike mink. Other normal fur breeds include the Argentés, Beverens and Siberians, most of which come in several colours, such as blue, black, white or cream. The Lilac is a shade of pinkish grey.

FANCY BREEDS

Over the years mutations have occurred (see p.45), giving the breeders a range of entirely new features to work with. Mutant changes of coat texture and pattern, of ears, of size and conformation, have produced breeds such as the grotesque-looking Lops, Netherland Dwarfs, tiny white Polish, huge Flemish Giants, the Belgian Hare (almost as large), Harlequins and Magpies. The Angora is the only rabbit bred for its wool, which can reach 12cm/5in in length.

New Zealand Red

Blue Beveren

Lop-Eared

Angora

Silver Fawns

Netherland Dwarf

Dutch rabbits (yellow and black)

Some of the most attractive rabbits, with distinctive body patterns quite unlike anything in the wild population are also classified as fancy breeds. They are the Dutch, English and Himalayan rabbits.

Dutch The Dutch is a small, bi-coloured rabbit of perhaps 2.2 kg/5 lb, with the well-known saddle marking. Originally a black and white rabbit, it is now bred in a range of colours including tortoiseshell, chocolate, yellow, blue and grey on a white ground.

English

English Equally striking is the English rabbit. This is a medium breed of about 3.6 kg/8 lb. The pattern consists of a butterfly-marked snout, a narrow saddle along the spine, dark ears, dark eye circles, cheek spots and chain markings on the flanks. Colours are blue, black, tortoiseshell, chocolate, or grey on white. Like the Dutch, this is a nineteenth-century breed, the result of mutation.

Orange Rex

Himalayan and Californian Early breeders produced a small, elegant rabbit, the Himalayan, weighing about 2.2 kg/5 lb, with coloured points like a Siamese cat. The points are usually black, but may also be blue or chocolate.

This 'Siamese' colourpointing proved very popular and the same pattern has been introduced much more recently among the normal fur breeds, with a type called the Californian. Although it has similar fur markings, the Californian cannot be confused with the Himalayan because it weighs twice as much.

REX AND SATIN BREEDS

The Rex and Satin rabbits are twentieth-century breeds. The Rex is characterized by short, dense fur that looks and feels like plush. It is the result of a mutant factor, first seen in France in 1919, that reduces the guard hairs to the length of the underhair.

About twenty years later the Satins were bred in America. The Satin sheen is the result of a mutant factor causing the fur to roll back. Rexes and Satins are bred in a range of colours, and cross with many of the other breeds to produce, for instance, the Chinchilla Rex. The Astrex is a curly-coated rabbit.

Himalayan

Rabbits in the wild

Rabbits have existed for millions of years, but Phoenician traders a thousand years ago were the first people to make a written record of the many timid little burrowing animals they saw in Spain.

Wild rabbits live in extended family groups in underground burrows called warrens. Tunnels link the sleeping and nesting chambers to the several exits. Warrens are often built on the edge of woodland bordering grass or arable fields. The rabbits doze in their burrows by day, then, in the early morning and at dusk, they venture into the fields to feed. They stamp their feet to warn of predators like hawks, stoats and foxes – and man.

A dominant female and her mate rule the other females and males in the warren. Most rabbit kittens are born in the spring when food is most abundant.

Biology

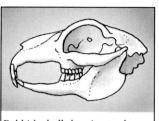

Rabbit's skull showing teeth

Lagomorphs Rabbits are classed as lagomorphs, not as rodents, as was once the case. A small order of mammals, the lagomorphs comprise the rabbits, *Oryctolagus*; the hares, *Lepus*; the pikas, *Ochotona*; and the cotton tails, *Sylvilagus*.

The name lagomorph is derived from two Greek words: *lagos* a hare, and *morphe*, meaning form or likeness. The distinguishing features of the lagomorphs include the habit of pseudo-rumination; the paired incisors in the upper jaw; the scut; the long, erect ears; hind limbs longer than the fore; and feeding without the use of the fore limbs.

Tail The rabbit's short tail, or scut, is a characteristic feature of the lagomorphs. It is so distinctive that the rabbit's American counterpart is known as the cotton tail.

The scut is upturned to show the pale hair on the underside, and the bucks carry their tails rather higher than the does. The scut is probably a useful biological signalling device: an obvious danger signal, but also a means by which rabbits grazing over a wide area can easily keep one another in sight.

Appendix The appendix, which is merely vestigial in man, is a well-developed and necessary part of the rabbit's alimentary canal. Together with all herbivores, the rabbit needs a long gut for the assimilation of its rather indigestible diet. Cellulose, which in man would be expelled as roughage, is broken down in the

Teeth The rabbit is, by nature, a grazing animal. Wild rabbits have played so significant a part in landscaping the countryside, particularly the chalk downlands and sandy heaths, that the sudden loss of rabbits in Britain in the 1950s from myxomatosis, resulted in some noticeable changes in vegetation.

The teeth are well adapted for this grazing habit. There are no canines, just incisors to bite off the vegetation, and premolars and molars to crush and grind it before swallowing. The incisors are particularly interesting because they are paired, one behind the other, in the upper jaw, giving 6

Tail or scut

rabbit's appendix and caecum by the bacterial activity. Even so, food needs to be passed twice through the body (see Pseudo-rumination).

incisors in the permanent set, whereas the rodents have only 4 incisors. This is the feature that once led biologists to classify the lagomorphs as 'double-toothed rodents'.

When gnawing, the cheeks are drawn into the diastema, the space between the incisors and the cheek teeth, and this forms a barrier to splinters.

Pseudo-rumination The rabbit has the habit, known as pseudo-rumination, of swallowing small soft pellets of partly digested food taken directly from the anus with the mouth. It compares with the ruminant animals chewing the cud, and allows for the better digestion of the herbivorous diet which is difficult to break down. Pseudo-rumination is normal lagomorph behaviour, and rabbits deprived of reingesting food in this way have died within weeks. Waste matter is finally expelled in hard faecal pellets such as those which wild rabbits deposit on old molehills.

Lop-eared rabbit

Ears By nature a rabbit has slim, erect ears which, in wild specimens, measure about 9cm/ 3½in. In general, the ears of tame rabbits are in proportion to the size of the breed – Polish and Netherland Dwarf rabbits have much shorter ears than the larger Flemish Giants and New Zealands. The ears can be pricked, not only to catch sounds, but also to expose a skin surface to the air for cooling the body. Lop-eared rabbits have been bred selectively to produce these extraordinarily aberrant ears. They can measure 17cm/7in across, and 72cm/28½in in length from tip to tip. Lop-ears are always carried in this position, hanging down uselessly, having lost all power of movement. They are so heavy that the skull shape has been altered by them, and both hearing and movement adversely affected.

Gait Rabbits have the characteristic loping gait of the lagomorphs, determined by the long hind limbs that make it impossible for them to walk or run. A rabbit at ease will move from one spot to the next with slow leap-frogging movements, but once alerted to danger, it can make a short, but very fast sprint to safety. At high speed the hind limbs are placed well before the fore limbs, making this easily recognizable V-shaped track.

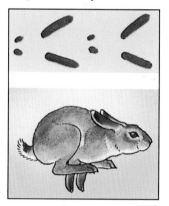

Feet Wild rabbits are accomplished burrowers, and given opportunity tame ones can dig sizeable runs for themselves. The earth is dug out with the fore limbs, and thrown backwards with the hind, a practice that tends to make a furrow-like entrance to the holes. In spite of the fact that most rabbits live underground, their feet have not become specialized for digging. They still resemble the feet of hares which live above ground, as some rabbits do, finding shelter in vegetation.

Rabbit's foot

Choosing a rabbit

It is easy to be bowled over by the first fluffy rabbit seen in a pet shop, but it is better to be prudent before buying.

AGE
The best age to acquire a rabbit is when it is between nine and twelve weeks old, when it will be easy to handle and tame.

HEALTH
A young rabbit in good condition when you acquire it will be less likely to present health problems – and mounting veterinary bills – later on. Ask to hold the rabbit and check over the following points (see also p.35):

The rabbit's coat should be sleek and glossy, the ears clean right the way down the inside, and the eyes bright. Claws should be neither too long nor torn at the ends, and the teeth also should be clean and not too long. There should be no visible wounds or abscesses on the body, and the back should be firm, without a protruding backbone.

Beware of any rabbit with a runny nose or diarrhoea – check for signs of diarrhoea, staining or matting of the fur under the tail. Equally, there should be no signs of discharge from eyes or nose, nor should the rabbit be sneezing. The fur around the nose and on the inside of the forelegs should not be matted.

BREED
Small and medium breeds like the Netherland Dwarf (about 1 kg/2–3 lb), the tiny Polish and Dutch (up to 2.5 kg/5½ lb) are usually better for the inexperienced rabbit-keeper or for children, rather than the heaviest breeds such as the Californian, the New Zealand White (shown here with a Netherland Dwarf) and the Flemish Giant.

SOURCES

Where to buy a rabbit depends partly on whether a pure-bred is wanted for showing, or whether a healthy, attractive pet will do just as well. A top quality show rabbit will have to be acquired from a specialist breeder, who can be contacted through rabbit clubs or by way of specialist magazines.

Many pet shops also sell rabbits. Often, but not invariably, these rabbits are of indeterminate breed. They may be 'seconds', disposed of for failing to meet the stringent requirements of the standard, or they may be crossbreeds. This does not matter to the pet keeper. Such animals can be attractive in their own right, appealing pets, and much less expensive to buy than recognized breeds.

What has to be considered is their health and background. Rabbits bred from stock that is old, immature, underfed, or exhausted by repeated breeding, tend to be small and frail themselves, and to produce weak and undersized offspring.

SEXING

Initially, it is best to acquire two females (see p.16), but if, any two rabbits are to live together, it is essential to check they are the appropriate sex, whether wanted for breeding or not. Even pet shop keepers have been known to make mistakes in sexing an animal, so, to be on the safe side, double check for yourself.

Sexing rabbit kittens The males have a round genital opening, and gentle pressure around it will expose the penis. The females have a genital slit.

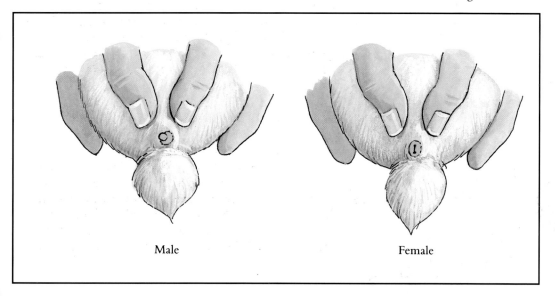

Male　　　　　　　Female

COMPANIONSHIP

One of a rabbit's greatest needs is for companionship. Rabbits are social animals in the wild, and in captivity are best kept in small groups. For this reason the females, the does, make better pets than the bucks. Two or three does are normally placid enough to live together peacefully, although a pregnant one would need her own hutch.

By contrast, all bucks need to be housed singly by the time they are three months old, though they should be able to see each other. From the age of puberty they are capable of mating the does, and are aggressive with each other, unless from the same litter and neutered. Temperament varies somewhat with breed, but in general the bucks are so assertive that rivalry between them leads to fierce fighting.

Rabbits and guinea pigs can be great friends, and live together amicably in the same hutch or run. Cats and rabbits brought up together can also tolerate each other well.

When a solitary rabbit is, nevertheless, kept as a pet, it will need and deserve a good deal of human contact, and preferably the contact of another animal. Sometimes rabbits can be kept with guinea pigs, poultry, tortoises or budgerigars, provided introductions are made when both animals are young.

Such associations of compatible animals are good, providing there is no bullying or worrying, and no obvious danger to health. Friendships between dogs and rabbits, or between cats and rabbits can also occur, but it is prudent to view these a little more suspiciously. The predatory nature of carnivores can show itself unexpectedly, though sometimes the tables are turned and a buck rabbit will chase a timid cat.

Belgian Hare doe with her four-weeks-old young

Dalmatian Rex

Chocolate Dutch doe with young

dagascan Dwarf also known as Sooty Fawn or Tortoiseshell

c young

Californian

The hutch

A good roomy hutch is absolutely basic to a rabbit's welfare. Well designed, properly constructed, and carefully maintained, it will serve for years, and probably for the rabbit's whole life.

Considering how much a rabbit can suffer if confined even in a good hutch, it is distressing to see how many are still kept in hopelessly outmoded and inadequate conditions. Quite commonly rabbits are housed in small, box-like cages, hung on a wall, or standing directly on the ground. Keeping rabbits alone and permanently caged condemns them to a life of unrelieved boredom, and shows appalling insensitivity to their nature, and ignorance of their needs.

Essentially a good hutch is divided into two connecting compartments: one for day with a wire mesh door to admit light and air; one fitted with a solid door to provide a retreat at night, and from wind, rain, snow and the cold.

Raising the hutch off the ground to table height also gives protection from rising damp, rats and dogs. It also simplifies cleaning, because the floor can be scraped towards the front edge, and the scrapings dropped down into a bucket.

The amount of cleaning necessary obviously depends on how much the hutch is used. Rabbits do urinate heavily, and daily cleaning will be essential if they are caged for long. A layer of absorbent paper beneath the litter on the floor of the hutch will help to keep the base dry, and sometimes a tray can be used in the day compartment for the same purpose. Rabbits are unlikely to soil their bedding, so that can be left undisturbed for much longer.

Correct siting of the hutch is important. It needs to be in a sheltered position, should not face directly into the mid-day sun, nor into the prevailing wind.

Rabbits are generally hardy, but need protection from extremes of temperature. In severe weather the hutch will need the additional shelter of an outhouse; in hot weather it will need moving into the shade. It can actually be very dangerous to shut rabbits into a hutch on a hot day, for they

Inadequate hutch   It is still all too common to see rabbits kept in small box-like hutches, such as this, often standing directly on the earth, and subject to rising damp and disturbance by rats and dogs. In general, it is not possible to convert a box into a hutch, which ideally should be built on a timber frame.

are liable to succumb to heat exhaustion (see p.39). If they must be caged, the hutch will need to be fully ventilated, with the roof propped open if possible, and frequently hosed down with cold water to reduce the temperature of the interior.

On cold or stormy nights the rabbits need the protection of a louvred panel which can be clipped into the framework of the day door. This gives extra protection from low temperatures, driving rain, and unaccustomed lights. Polythene sheeting can do the same job, provided there is also good ventilation.

The needs of a rabbit like this black and tan are not difficult to supply: fresh food, a chance to graze, companionship – and the security of a warm, clean hutch.

Size The minimum size of hutch for two small or medium-sized rabbits is 150 × 60 × 60cm/60 × 24 × 24in. Two large-sized rabbits will need a hutch measuring 180 × 90 × 90cm/72 × 36 × 36in.

Gnawing block Rabbits will damage their own hutch by gnawing in order to wear down their incisor teeth. This damage can usually be avoided by giving them a bark-covered log for use as a gnawing block.

Food dishes The best food pots for rabbits are heavy earthenware ones which can be scalded between feeds and which are not easily overturned. Plastic pots are much less satisfactory. Rabbits tend to play with them and gnaw them, especially when confined to the hutch and suffering boredom.

Bedding The sleeping compartment needs a layer of newspaper covered by a layer of peat moss litter, cat litter or wood chippings, about 5cm/2in deep, with a deep layer of straw on top. In severe weather it should be possible for the rabbits to sleep inside an entire bale of straw.

A shelf in the sleeping compartment allows a nursing doe to rest away from her litter from time to time.

Doors The hutch needs separate doors to the day and sleeping compartments, both well fitting with good hinges and catches. A louvred panel (p.21), made to fit, within the frame of the day door, is a very useful addition.

Exterior The exterior of the hutch may be protected with gloss paint or polyurethane varnish. Do not paint inside, in case the paint is not safe for gnawing.

The roof   The roof needs to be covered with roofing felt for good weatherproofing, and should overhang the hutch to keep its sides dry and to prevent driving rain from saturating the interior. It is also important to pitch the roof towards the back where it may be hinged for better ventilation on very hot days.

Hay rack   To avoid its being trampled underfoot and soiled the rabbits' daily supply of hay is best given in a hay rack in the hutch.

Water bottle   Drinking water, which must always be available to the rabbits, is usually given in a drip-fed bottle fixed to the side of the hutch or to the wire mesh of the day compartment door. Water provided in pots tends to be spilled and soiled quickly.

Floor litter   As in the sleeping compartment, the floor of the day compartment needs a layer of litter spread of top of newspaper that will absorb the urine.

Ramp   A ramp, or a flight of steps, can be placed in front of the opened door during the day to allow the rabbits free exercise within their own enclosure. At night the rabbits should be shut in the hutch for safety and the ramp moved away.

Construction   The best construction is tongued and grooved boarding on a timber frame. The interior should be lined for added insulation, and to cover the framework which if left exposed, will be gnawed by the rabbits.

Height   A hutch should be raised to table height on legs, or on a base, to give protection from rising damp, other animals, such as marauding dogs, and to make cleaning out easier. It should stand slightly away from an adjacent wall to allow free air circulation, and to prevent rats and mice lodging there.

Cleaning   If the door to the day compartment opens to leave no ledge at the front of the hutch floor, cleaning is made easy. But a breeding hutch does need a (removable) board, so young rabbits cannot fall out.

A rabbit enclosure

The diversity of form among rabbit breeds should not be allowed to obscure the fact that tame rabbits differ from their wild forebears only in superficial ways. No matter how highly bred they may be, in biology and in habit they remain very close to the wild.

In captivity rabbits need an environment where their life style can approximate to the natural, if only on a much reduced scale. In particular they must have a certain amount of physical freedom so that it is possible for them to hop around, and preferably to dig in the earth and to graze. It has to be remembered that a wild rabbit may cover several miles a day. Consequently the great challenge facing rabbit owners is how to provide

This is a simple method of linking the mesh panels of a rabbit enclosure. Screw-eyes bought from a hardware shop and hinge pins (easily made from a wire coathanger), will enable you to alter the shape and position of the enclosure to suit circumstances and to allow the rabbit access to fresh grass. The lower pin should be made long enough to stake the panel firmly into the ground.

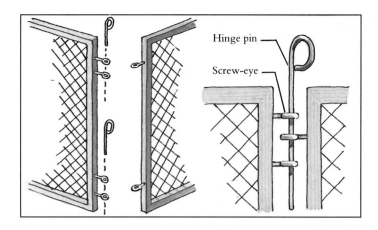

Hinge pin

Screw-eye

By siting the hutch within an enclosure, rabbits can be given a certain amount of freedom each day. On bare earth, many rabbits will dig a bolt hole within the enclosure, and all should be given drain pipes to use as substitute burrows, also logs for climbing and for gnawing blocks.

A flight of steps or a ramp will allow the rabbits to exercise out of the hutch and to retreat back to their sleeping compartment at will during the day. At night they must be shut into the hutch for safety.

safe yet stimulating surroundings for their pets. Probably the best solution is to site the rabbit hutch within an enclosure. During the day the hutch door can be left open, and by the use of a ramp or a flight of steps, the rabbits can be left free to come and go as they like.

Sometimes the entire garden can be used as the enclosure, being safely walled or fenced, and so laid out that all-round observation is possible. However, a free-ranging rabbit will not distinguish between weeds and choice seedlings. In particular, rabbits seem to relish digging up (though not necessarily eating) recently planted subjects, and their scrabbles and scrapes in flower beds and lawn make for friction with keen gardeners. So a rabbit should only be allowed to run free in a 'natural' garden or in a part dedicated to its use.

When, as happens much more often, the garden as a whole is unsuitable, it will be necessary to partition off a section. With this idea in mind, a careful survey is almost certain to reveal a possible site, and quite probably some existing feature, such as a wall, that can be incorporated into the enclosure. New fencing will need to be at least 1 m/ 3 ft high – higher if it also has to keep dogs out – and sunk into the ground to prevent escape by burrowing. A concrete sill should prevent tunnelling under the gate.

It often happens that it is comparatively easy to enclose a paved area, and there are the added advantages of having a surface that can be sluiced down quickly, and one that soon dries after rain. It seems cruel, nevertheless, to deprive rabbits of all contact with the earth. Allow periods of free exercise in the garden, or use a paved enclosure in conjunction with a portable exercise run, such as an ark (see p.29).

Feeding

As herbivores, rabbits need a diet consisting almost entirely of vegetable matter. It will contain a full range of proteins, fats, and carbohydrates, together with vitamins and minerals, but the proteins and fats will be those of vegetable origin, such as are found in wheat. This diet can be enriched by milk and by providing a mineral lick bought from a pet shop.

Young rabbits enjoying a meal of pellet food.

A good mash is a mixture of flaked maize, crushed oats, mixed corn, rabbit pellets, and bran, made into a crumbly mash with hot water or milk, or fed dry.

An alternative is wholemeal bread, made into a mash with hot or cold milk, and possibly with an added measure of bran. White bread should not be fed, and rabbits who dislike a mash and prefer dry food, should have their wholemeal bread toasted or baked hard in the oven.

A substantial meal like this should normally be fed once a day, or more when necessary, for instance for pregnant or nursing does.

In nature all the herbivores spend a great deal of time feeding, and captive rabbits similarly need the activity it provides. This is the reason highly concentrated foods such as pellets, although nutritionally balanced, are best fed with plenty of fresh foods, and with hay. Hay of the best quality is a staple food for rabbits, and should be fed to them daily. For hygienic reasons it is best given in a hay rack, rather than put on the hutch floor, where it will become trampled and soiled. A rack of hay each day will allow rabbits to feed sporadically throughout their waking hours, as in nature.

Good hygiene needs to be considered. Besides using a rack for hay, caring owners find it most satisfactory to put mash in heavy, earthenware pots that are easy to wash, and to use a drip-feed bottle for drinking water.

In addition to their mash, rabbits will need another meal each day consisting of greenstuffs, vegetables and fruits. Suitable fresh foods include apples, Brussels sprouts, cabbage, carrots, cauliflower, celery, chicory, kale, lettuce, parsnip, pears, peas and their pods, spinach, swede, and turnip.

Rabbits will eat many of the wild plants collected from the countryside, such as agrimony, coltsfoot, comfrey, cow parsnip, goosegrass, hedge parsley, knapweed, shepherd's purse, and sow thistle. They will also graze grass and its associated weeds including plantain, chickweed, dandelion, and clover. It is vital that any grazing area or greenfood offered should not have been polluted with weedkiller, fertilizer or any other toxic substance.

Very few greenfoods harm rabbits, unless fed in vast quantities. It is, however, a mistake to give a complete feed of one particular greenstuff, and far safer to mix different plants. Coarse lush greenstuff grown in shade should not be fed, nor should plants that are mildewed, dirty, or attacked by blight or fungus.

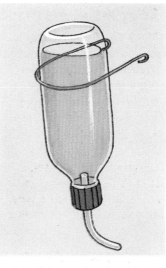

A drip-fed water bottle with a stainless steel spout is the best way of offering drinking water to a rabbit.

A mineral lick should be attached securely to the hutch bars or wire mesh, to make it easily available at all times.

Suggested diet chart

	What?	When?	How much?
Medium-sized rabbit (vary quantities for larger or smaller breeds)	whole crushed oats or wheat *or* mash *or*	} morning	50g/1¾oz 50g/1¾oz
	rabbit pellets	1–2 times a week	50g/1¾oz
	mixed fresh greens washed in cold water	evening	170g/6oz
	fresh water mineral lick hay	} always available	
	whole apple or carrot	2–3 times a week	
Pregnant doe (during 30–33 days gestation period)	As above, but gradually increase amounts until receiving *twice* normal feed by end of gestation period.		
Nursing doe	As above, but increasing amount until receiving *three* times normal feed by end of lactation period (6–8 weeks after birth of kittens). Then slowly cut back on doe's food, returning to normal amount several weeks after kittens are weaned.		
Growing kittens	see p. 42.		

Something that puzzles many people new to rabbit-keeping is the rabbit's habit of eating its soft droppings. This is called pseudo-rumination and is quite normal – see p.12.

Even if the rabbits cannot safely be let out into the garden to feed, they can be allowed some controlled grazing by the use of a portable ark (opposite). This is constructed of wire mesh on a timber frame of triangular shape, with a roof at one end. Wire mesh on the base may not be necessary, except for accomplished burrowers, unless the frame is so light that the rabbits, or dogs, can overturn it. Re-positioning the run each day will provide fresh grazing. Such an ark, however, is for temporary use only and no substitute for a hutch, though it must have a sheltered area with hay for cover as a retreat from disturbance, rain or cold.

WARNING
Wild plants which should definitely *not* be fed to rabbits include:

anemone
wild arum
autumn crocus
bindweed
bluebells
bryony
buttercup
(though harmless
when dried)
celandine
dog mercury
elder
figwort
fool's parsley
foxglove
hemlock
(very easily confused
with hedge parsley)
henbane
any of the nightshades
poppy
toadflax
traveller's joy (wild clematis)

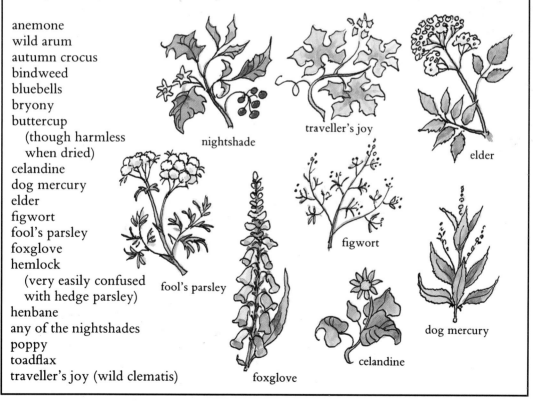

nightshade

traveller's joy

elder

fool's parsley

figwort

foxglove

celandine

dog mercury

Cleaning the hutch

Good hygiene will not only make sure the rabbit is comfortable but help to keep it healthy. Any rabbit will do far better in a clean, sweet-smelling hutch than in a dirty one.

Rabbits are naturally very clean animals, and unless confined for a long period or not cleaned out sufficiently often, will tend to use one corner only as a lavatory. However, they do urinate heavily and the smell of the urine can be very strong. Whether a hutch smells or not is entirely up to the rabbit-keeper. If any rabbit has, unfortunately, to be confined to its hutch for a long period, the hutch will need cleaning daily. A cleaning routine such as that outlined opposite will ensure the hutch is kept healthy and comfortable.

Rabbit droppings make good fertilizer, so litter and bedding are an excellent addition to the compost heap. With no heap available, it is probably best to burn old bedding, though in a smokeless zone it must be carefully packed and sealed in plastic bags.

In summertime a few drops of *mild* disinfectant (not phenol-based) sprinkled on the hutch floor before fresh litter is added will discourage flies, which can cause health risks (see p.38).

Three to four times a year the hutch should be washed and disinfected, then rinsed off well and allowed to dry thoroughly before the rabbit is put back. If a hutch is empty for any time, it should be well scrubbed out with a strong solution of household ammonia to kill any germs lingering in the cracks of the wood. When dry, the *outside* of the hutch can be creosoted or limewashed, and again allowed to dry thoroughly before it houses more rabbits. The inside should not be treated in this way, in case the rabbits gnaw the wood and are poisoned. However, if serious disease strikes, it is best to burn the hutch rather than run the risk of installing more rabbits in it.

Any concrete area in a permanent run should be hosed down from time to time. Grass within a portable run should be lightly dusted with lime after it has been nibbled down and that area not re-used until a really good crop of grass has grown again. Using the same patch two or three times a year is quite sufficient. More frequent use may give the rabbit stomach upsets.

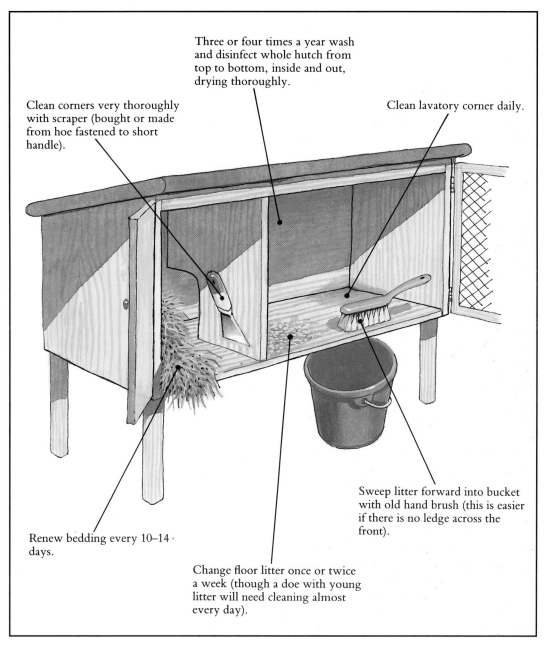

Three or four times a year wash and disinfect whole hutch from top to bottom, inside and out, drying thoroughly.

Clean corners very thoroughly with scraper (bought or made from hoe fastened to short handle).

Clean lavatory corner daily.

Renew bedding every 10–14 days.

Change floor litter once or twice a week (though a doe with young litter will need cleaning almost every day).

Sweep litter forward into bucket with old hand brush (this is easier if there is no ledge across the front).

Grooming and handling

Rabbits regularly groom themselves, and with one notable exception are capable of keeping their fur in tiptop condition. Providing their health is good, their food right, and their living quarters clean, rabbits' coats will have a natural gloss.

The exception is the Angora, one of the oldest and most popular breeds, whose unique wool coat can grow to a length of 12 cm/5 in, and needs a great deal of attention. Angoras are, however, charming, docile rabbits which will submit to being brushed frequently. They should be kept only by enthusiasts who can accept that meticulous grooming is a normal part of the daily routine.

For all the remaining breeds, whether other fancy varieties, normal fur breeds, or Rex and Satin breeds, grooming is not strictly necessary. Even show rabbits may have no more than a burnish with a silk scarf.

Grooming a rabbit   Except for the long-haired Angora, grooming rabbits is not strictly necessary for the coat, but is valuable because it gives the handler opportunity to observe the animal's condition and encourages the rabbit to become tame. Associations with other animals give rabbits companionship, but must be supervised if there is any threat to the rabbit's safety.

Given adequate accommodation, rabbits will keep themselves and most of the living space clean. It is only when infrequently cleaned out that their fur may become soiled. However, bathing would not be necessary, although there may be occasional need to wash a section of fur.

Even so, regular brushing is recommended. It removes loose hairs during the summer months when the heavy winter coat is being moulted, and the rabbits respond well to attention from their owners. They tend to become tamer, easier to handle and much more companionable.

During grooming, the caring owner will take the opportunity of checking over the rabbit's condition. It is a particularly good time to take note of the weight, and to examine the rabbit for the signs of health listed on p.35.

Rabbits are so often badly handled, that it is worth while for a family to discuss the problem, and to decide how best to pick up their own rabbits. It helps if the handling method is consistent, and if the rabbits are handled frequently.

When lifting, it is essential to take the animal's weight on one arm, and to steady the rabbit by gently grasping the scruff of the neck or the base of the ears. It is clearly monstrous to attempt to lift the weight of a rabbit by the ears alone. Once in the arms, the rabbit can be cradled, or held against the body with its head over one shoulder.

Holding a rabbit Rabbits should be handled frequently if they are to become tame. They should never be lifted by the ears or by the scruff of the neck, but with two hands and then cradled against the handler's body.

On returning a rabbit to its hutch the best method is to lower it in hind feet first. It is then impossible for the rabbit to kick out and inflict a scratch on the handler. Children cannot be expected to lift safely any rabbits other than the small and medium breeds.

The healthy rabbit

Clean food, clean water, clean bedding and clean hutches will in most cases keep rabbits healthy. Examining, handling and grooming a rabbit every day will also play a major part in its health. Knowing how a rabbit looks and acts when it is well will make it easier to recognize quickly any change for the worse in its appearance or behaviour.

Rabbits should be examined regularly and carefully, especially the ears, eyes, nose and sexual organs. The list opposite will help check all is well.

No rabbit should be allowed to get fat. Obesity, like so many rabbit disorders, is the result of poor management. Rabbits shut up for long periods in a confined space are most at risk. They need far more freedom to exercise, and possibly a small adjustment to their diet: more greenstuffs, and less high calorie foods such as grains, balanced food pellets and bread.

Young Chocolate Dutch rabbits

The largest breeds tend to develop a dewlap under the chin. Does are most prone to this, and although the dewlap may look ominously like a goitre, it is in fact a roll of fatty tissue. A small one is to be expected in breeds as large as the New Zealand White and the Flemish Giant. Smaller breeds should maintain their neat build throughout life.

If there is any doubt about a rabbit's health, it should be taken to the vet immediately. Many illnesses and parasites (see pp.37-9) can easily be cured, especially in their early stages.

SIGNS OF HEALTH

Abdomen	free from wounds, sores: not distended.
Anus	clean, with no staining, scouring or sores.
Appetite	good, both eating and drinking normally.
Breathing	quiet and regular.
Claws	short and not torn at the ends.
Coat	smooth, glossy and clean, with no bare patches or parasites.
Demeanour	alert and watchful, even at rest.
Droppings	dry and well-formed.
Ears	clean, free from scabs and deposits; pricked to the slightest sound (except Lops).
Eyes	clear, bright and watchful, with no discharge.
Feet	strong, clean feet, with no cysts between the toes, or soreness of the hocks. No matted fur on soles.
Movement	strong movements, particularly in the hind legs.
Nose	twitching rhythmically, with no discharge.
Skin	clean, supple, without abscesses, ringworm, wounds, scurf, inflammation or sores of any kind.
Teeth	clean and of normal length.

OVERGROWN CLAWS

Owners often wisely let a vet or an experienced rabbit keeper clip their rabbit's claws the first time, but it is not difficult. With a pair of animal nail clippers from a pet shop, the claw should be cut straight across, taking care not to cut into the blood and nerve supply. In a pale coloured rabbit this can be seen by holding the paw to the light. With a dark coloured rabbit a cautious cut should take off only a small amount of claw.

OVERGROWN TEETH

A rabbit's front teeth continue to grow and need wearing down on hard food and a gnawing block, preferably a newly cut log with the bark left on. Otherwise, the teeth may grow so long as to lever the jaws slowly apart or lock into the opposite jaw. Stems of kale and Brussels sprouts, as well as root vegetables, are good hard food.

When you are away

Either the rabbit must be boarded out with a pet shop, vet, or other suitable and knowledgeable person, or someone must come in twice a day to give the rabbit food and water, and to shut it in at night. Such a person must be prepared to clean out the hutch if the arrangement lasts for more than a few days. It should go without saying that the rabbit must never be left to its own devices for any length of time, even with an adequate supply of food.

A tough cardboard box can be used for transporting a rabbit to the veterinary surgery, provided its lid is secured and holes are punched in the sides for ventilation. The larger rabbits can be very strong, however, and many owners find it safer and more convenient to keep a cat basket for any necessary trips to the vet.

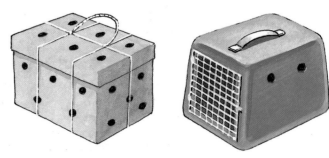

Ailments and parasites

Coccidiosis A microscopic, internal parasite is responsible for this common, but very serious disease of the liver. The organism is present in the faecal pellets, and so can be transmitted from one rabbit to another, and particularly from a doe to her kittens, in a dirty hutch. Symptoms of coccidiosis are a yellow jaundiced look, persistent diarrhoea and extreme weakness. Without treatment the rabbit becomes emaciated, yet develops a pot-bellied appearance due to enlargement of the liver. Death is due to exhaustion.

It is necessary to isolate a suspected case of coccidiosis, and to seek veterinary help immediately. Drugs can effectively control the disease if it is diagnosed and treated professionally without delay.

Constipation and diarrhoea Constipation may be a simple dietary disorder, cured by feeding more greenstuffs; diarrhoea may be cured by withholding greens for twenty-four hours and feeding only hay and water. When persistent, or when combined with other symptoms, both conditions may indicate more serious illness needing veterinary diagnosis.

Fleas Rabbits which are seen to display symptoms of discomfort and irritation that make them scratch, may be infested with fleas. These tend to cluster around the head, and particularly the neck, where the dark spots of their excreta may be noticed. Fleas can be destroyed by the application of an insecticide powder sold by chemists for this purpose.

Fleas reproduce by laying eggs in the host animal's bedding, or on the floor. It is therefore impossible to eradicate them without burning every last straw of the bedding and the floor litter, scrubbing out the hutch and grazing ark and thoroughly sluicing down all other areas in use. Any crack can harbour the eggs, and in a few days – two to twelve in summer, longer in winter – the larvae will emerge, and the life cycle begins again.

European with myxomatosis

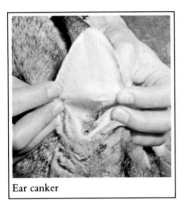

Ear canker

The rabbit flea has achieved some notoriety over the last thirty or so years as carrier of the virus that causes **myxomatosis**. During an outbreak the great majority of tame rabbits are safe. Veterinary advice should be taken about any felt to be at risk on account of the proximity of wild rabbits. An injection of vaccine will give immunity within three days and last approximately one year.

Flystrike   A major summer problem for long-haired rabbits is the 'strike fly' which lays its eggs in faeces-soiled fur. Within 12 to 24 hours, the maggots hatch out and bore into the host's flesh, ultimately killing the rabbit. Prevention is essential, so the rabbit should be checked daily to ensure the area under its tail is clean. Hutches should be cleaned out every day and fresh bedding provided.

Lice   Discomfort and scratching, as with fleas, can be caused by an infestation of lice. Unlike fleas, lice lay their eggs – known as nits – in the fur of the animal host. The eggs are white and secured to the fur by a natural adhesive. They show up particularly well on dark-coated rabbits, but will be noticed on any fur during grooming.

Lice can be destroyed by a specially prepared insecticide powder supplied by a chemist or veterinary surgeon. It is effective, however, only when the maker's instructions are followed exactly. Several applications are necessary to eliminate the succeeding generations of lice emerging from the nits.

Mites   Rabbits are frequently troubled by several different mites. The ear mite can cause a condition generally known as ear mange, or ear canker. Any rabbit showing symptoms of irritation and distress that make it scratch the ears and shake the head, or those with a powdery brown matter in the ears need prompt veterinary treatment.

Forage and harvest mites also attack rabbits. They burrow into the skin and set up an area of intense irritation that the rabbit will scratch until it is raw. This condition, usually known as mange, must also receive veterinary treatment.

Pneumonia   A rabbit huddled in a corner with laboured breathing, loss of appetite, a lacklustre coat, and often a discharge from its nose probably has pneumonia. The rabbit should be immediately seen by a vet. Pneumonia is often caused by damp hutches or bedding.

Snuffles   A respiratory tract condition, similar to the common cold in man, is known throughout the rabbit world as snuffles. This is a highly infectious disease, and the danger is that it may lead to pneumonia. Rabbits sneezing and with a discharge from the nose should be isolated well away from other rabbits and veterinary help sought.

Ticks   Sometimes ticks attach themselves to rabbits and feed on their blood for several days. Once fully engorged, the ticks will drop off naturally, but they cannot be pulled off whole while still alive. The head remains firmly in position. They can be killed by cutting off their air supply with a smear of vaseline, fat or butter. Afterwards it is possible to pull them away cleanly using a pair of tweezers.

First Aid

It is always advisable to isolate a sick rabbit, and to take prompt veterinary advice. Rabbits have poor recuperative powers, and immediate veterinary attention is imperative if they are to recover. Time should not be wasted attempting home cures or using patent remedies, before seeking veterinary help. As a general rule, the rabbit should be kept warm and given water to stop it dehydrating (a dropper is useful for this).

Accidents   The rabbit should be picked up carefully in the usual way (wrapped in an old towel if it is likely to struggle), and taken immediately to the vet. A cat basket makes an ideal rabbit carrier, or, at a pinch, a strong grocery box pierced with airholes, and secured with a lid or string.

Heatstroke   Rabbits can suffer quite easily from heatstroke if confined to small, badly ventilated and unshaded hutches in very hot weather. The rabbit should be put immediately in a cool, shady place and given plenty of water to drink, as well as hay and good greenfood. The fur over the shoulders should be moistened with a damp cloth.

Wounds   Wounds are usually inflicted as a result of two rabbits fighting. The combatants should be given separate quarters and the wounds bathed with a mild saline solution. Serious wounding needs veterinary attention, for if such a wound is not well cleansed, an abscess may result.

A wet cloth over the shoulders helps cool an overheated rabbit.

Reproduction

Every rabbit keeper should think twice before any rabbit is allowed to breed. Unless good homes can definitely be found for its offspring, it is unkind and irresponsible to breed from pet rabbits. From the age of three to four months a doe can have up to 24 young a year. Even though

New Zealand White with mixed litter

it is not advisable to breed from her after three years old, that is still a frightening number of kittens.

Oestrus   The rabbit has no regular cycle of heat, or oestrus. Instead, the doe in breeding condition can ovulate at any time in response to the advances of a buck, and particularly in summer when environmental factors are favourable.

Birth control   The doe's ability to become pregnant perhaps ten times a year, makes it impossible to let the sexes run together without risk of their breeding.

Segregation of bucks and does is the simplest and usual method of birth control. Veterinary opinion should be sought about any other method. It is possible to neuter bucks, but this is usually done to stop them fighting among themselves. Castrated males may be attacked by females unless introduced under supervision, and on neutral ground. Vasectomized males are liable to induce pseudo-pregnancies in the females – see below.

Mating   To mate a doe it is necessary either to introduce her to the buck's hutch, or to introduce them on neutral ground. In her own quarters she is fiercely territorial and is liable to attack him.

Mating usually takes place within a few minutes, and they should be left together for a second mounting. An unresponsive female, not yet in breeding condition, can be reintroduced on another occasion, or mated to a different buck.

Pseudopregnancy   Pseudo, or false pregnancy, is a common condition among rabbits. It happens most often after an unsuccessful mating. The doe develops genuine symptoms of pregnancy, culminating in nest building. Pseudo-pregnancies can last from 10 to 23 days, most usually about 17 days.

Pregnancy   A true pregnancy lasts from 28 to 34 days, usually 31 days. During this time the pregnant doe needs isolation from the buck and all other rabbits, an increasing diet, and nest-building materials. By the time she gives birth to her young, her own diet will need to be twice the normal. Three weeks later, when suckling a whole litter of kittens, she will need three times her usual amount of food.

The young

Young rabbits are born, usually at night, blind, deaf, furless and completely helpless save for their ability to suckle. They are entirely dependent on the doe who, undisturbed, will tend them admirably. Understandably she is anxious, and on the defensive, and resents any interference at all.

Owners should curb their impatience to have a peep at the new-born kittens for fear it should have a disastrous effect on the doe's behaviour. It sometimes happens that a doe will cull a litter, apparently to remove weaklings, or to reduce the number of young she has to feed if her milk supply is insufficient. A doe will also kill normal kittens if they or the nest are disturbed.

In the wild the young rabbits spend their first weeks underground in a nursery burrow, stopped off from the rest of the warren and visited only by the doe for suckling. In captivity it will be perhaps three weeks before they emerge voluntarily from their nest in the doe's sleeping compartment into the daylight.

By this time they are fully furred, with ears and eyes open, and attempting to nibble at tender greens and hay. Their main nourishment will remain their dam's milk, and the doe will continue to suckle them for another three to five weeks, but they will show an increasing interest in solid food from now on. Offer as wide a variety of food as possible: green leaves, young root vegetables, mash and hay, as well as a little wholemeal bread and milk. A basic rule of thumb is to feed to appetite, but it is important that any food not eaten straight away is removed, so that the little rabbits do not get a chance to tread in and soil it. By the age of eight weeks the young litter will be fully weaned on to an adult diet, although in smaller amounts than a fully grown rabbit would consume.

At eight weeks the kittens are almost irresistible, with all the perfection of the miniature. Between now and twelve weeks is the best age to buy, when they are such a pleasure to handle that they quickly become tame, and a delight to the whole family.

But, beautiful and endearing as they are, the kittens should be resisted unless one has a mind to keep them imaginatively and well in a rabbit enclosure (p.24) that allows for physical freedom while keeping them safe. The more freedom and interest a rabbit has, the better it will respond and the more fun it will be as a pet. To reduce these rabbit kittens to mere backyard prisoners is unthinkable.

Two grey-white young

Your questions answered

My rabbits are free to roam most of the garden, which has been made escape-proof, but one rabbit in particular is nervous and difficult to catch. How can I make her tamer?

Some rabbits are more nervous than others and take a long time to become accustomed to handling – which is the first step towards being caught happily. If the rabbit is still quite young, and you are always patient with her, the situation should gradually improve. Never frighten her by chasing after her, and handle her frequently, so she becomes used to you and realizes she is not going to be hurt.

If the rabbit is much older and set in her ways, you may have more of a problem. Try putting her food in a hutch within a run at the same time every day, and she may go regularly into the enclosure for it. You can then shut the door on her, which will at least contain her. Keep on trying to tame her by frequent handling.

It is especially important to accustom rabbits to human contact if neighbours occasionally look after them. No rabbit-minder relishes crawling for hours through undergrowth!

The back claws of my young rabbit regularly split lengthways. Although this does not seem to inconvenience him, what should I do?

The most likely problem is that the claws are overlong and need trimming. Do not try to do the job yourself the first time, but watch a vet to see how it is done. Then carry on clipping them yourself whenever they need it.

How can I stop my rabbits being frightened by fireworks?

Most people remember that dogs and cats may be frightened by fireworks, but rabbits and other hutch animals are often forgotten. Obviously, you should never let off fireworks in your garden. You might move the rabbits' hutch into a shed or basement, but some experts would say that moving is just as unsettling for the rabbits as the fireworks. A louvred panel (p. 21) or a hessian sack over the hutch front, providing it is well ventilated, will be protection from firework flashes.

My rabbit hutch is in a sheltered part of the garden and the rabbits seem happy in it all winter, but on frosty mornings their water bottle is often frozen solid. What should I do?
If the water freezes only *occasionally* in very severe weather, put a pair of thick socks over the bottle to act as insulation. *Regular* freezing suggests the hutch is not sufficiently sheltered and should perhaps be moved into an outhouse such as a shed. Do not put it in a garage as car fumes are injurious to rabbits and may even kill them.

Rather than keeping solitary animals, we have a rabbit and a guinea pig, which we understood were usually compatible. But the rabbit keeps attacking and biting the guinea pig. Have we made a bad mistake?
Possibly you did not introduce the two animals when young. Equally, when introducing them, it is best to let them smell each other through cage bars or wires for 24 hours or so. Then let the larger animal into the cage of the smaller, so the former will feel slightly offguard out of its familiar territory.

It is also possible that the rabbit, if a male, is trying to mate the guinea pig. Or you may just be unlucky with these two – sometimes, despite doing all the right things some animals just will not get along.

After breeding with a white buck, my white doe has just had a litter in which one of the kittens is black. Why?
Each hereditary characteristic, like colour, shape or size, is determined by a pair of genes, one inherited from the buck, one from the doe. With similar genetic information from both parents, a rabbit develops like them. Dissimilar information may make it different or, if similar, the next generation may not breed true. So either your white doe or your white buck has a black rabbit somewhere among its ancestors.

Sometimes genes will change, or mutate, to create a new breed.

Life history

Scientific name	*Oryctolagus cunicuhis*
Gestation period	31 days (approx.)
Name of young	kitten
Litter size	6–8 (average)
Birth weight	30 g/1 oz–70 g/2½ oz
Eyes open	8–10 days
Weaning age	42–56 days
Weaning weight	300 g/10 oz– 800 g/1 lb 12 oz
Puberty	90 days – small breeds 120+ days – large breeds
Adult weight	1 kg/2 lb 4 oz–9 kg/20 lb
Best age to breed	120+ days – smaller breeds 300+ days – large breeds
Oestrus (or season)	any time, in response to stimulus from male
Retire from breeding	males 3–4 years females 2–3 years
Life expectancy	6-8 years

Record card

Record sheet for your own rabbits

<table>
<tr>
<td>(photograph or portrait)</td>
<td>(photograph or portrait)</td>
</tr>
</table>

Name _____

Date of birth
(actual or estimated) _____

Breed _____ Sex _____

Colour/description _____

Name _____

Date of birth
(actual or estimated) _____

Breed _____ Sex _____

Colour/description _____

Feeding notes _____

_____

_____

_____

_____

_____

_____

_____

Medical notes _____

_____

_____

_____

_____

_____

_____

_____

Veterinary Surgeon's name _____

Practice address _____

_____

Surgery hours _____

_____

Tel. no. _____

Index